The Battle of

Chesterfield

1266

Rupert Matthews

Acknowledgements

Photos, illustrations and maps are by the publisher except: Peveril Castle - Steven Newton; New Beetwell Street - Paullo; old post resturant - BazzaDaRambler; chesterfield long view = jon bennett; St Mary Church - gillbean; Ferrers arms as earl of derby - archetype1; tomb of adrian v - ALESSANDROMARCOA

Website - www.BretwaldaBooks.com
Twitter - @Bretwaldabooks
Facebook - Bretwalda Books
Blog - bretwaldabooks.blogspot.co.uk/

Bretwalda Books
Unit 8, Fir Tree Close, Epsom,
Surrey KT17 3LD
info@BretwaldaBooks.com
www.BretwaldaBooks.com
ISBN 978-1-909099-63-0

CONTENTS

Introduction   4

Chapter 1 The March to Chesterfield   5

Chapter 2 Leaders at Chesterfield   15

Chapter 3 Men, Weapons and Tactics   19

Chapter 4 The Battle of Chesterfield   29

Chapter 5 Aftermath   44

INTRODUCTION

The Battle of Chesterfield was fought in the later stages of the Baron's War, a civil war fought in England between 1264 and 1267. The sheer savagery of what happened in Chesterfield was rooted in that struggle. The major battles of Lewes and Evesham had already been fought, but the war was far from over as the countryside remained in turmoil and nobles were still choosing which side to support.

The town of Chesterfield was then a fairly minor market town, but it occupied a strategic position astride roads leading to York, Derby, North Wales and Lincolnshire. Not only that but it was perched on top of a spur of high ground between two swift rivers and so could be easily defended. Into this walled town came the rebel Robert de Ferrers, Earl of Derby, and his army. Derby was expecting reinforcements from Yorkshire, but they had not yet arrived.

Meanwhile, advancing from the south came Prince Henry of Almain with a larger royalist force. Henry knew where Derby was, but he had no idea where the rebel reinforcements might be, nor how many there were. There were, in fact, no less than four armies manoeuvring around Chesterfield in the middle of May 1266, none of which was entirely certain where the others were nor how strong they were.

The armies would meet in Chesterfield in a battle of great savagery and merciless violence. It was to be one of the most unusual battles of the middle ages as it was waged through the streets of the town, largely after dark and with the men fighting by the light of burning houses. When it was over the streets of Chesterfield ran red with blood and were piled high with the dead and the wounded. The defences of the town had been found wanting and would need replacing.

But although Henry of Almain had won a victory for King Henry III the underlying discontent had not gone away. The royal government would have to give way before peace came to England. And Henry himself had sown the seeds of his own destruction, sparking an act of savage revenge that would come years later and many miles away.

CHAPTER 1
THE MARCH TO CHESTERFIELD

The Barons War that led to the Battle of Chesterfield had erupted in 1264, but its roots reached back over half a century. It proved to be a civil war of enormous importance, far more so than the rather better known Wars of the Roses, for while the war did not lead to a change of ruler or dynasty it did profoundly alter the way in which England was governed, and we still live with those changes today.

A copy of the Magna Carta, bearing the seal of King John attached to a ribbon underneath. At the time it was agreed and for generations afterwards, Magna Carta was considered to be a touchstone of English liberty for nobles and freemen. Although most of its provisions were fairly arcane measures to stop royal abuse of feudal custom and suzerainty issues that affected only the nobles, whether or not a king was prepared to abide by the great charter or not was thought to be a key indicator of how much he would respect the rights of his citizens. It was the rejection of Magna Carta by King Henry III that laid the foundations for the civil war that was to follow.

In 1215 King John was forced to confirm the document known as Magna Carta by his rebellious barons. John had been ruling England as a despot, supported by foreign mercenaries. The great charter forced on him by the barons contained many clauses, but the key provision was that even the king had to obey the laws of the land. In dealing with his subjects the king could not arbitrarily imprison, fine or execute at will but only if the person had committed a crime. The weakness of Magna Carta, carefully drafted though it was, was that there was no mechanism to force the king to keep his promises and abide by the charter. However, the civil

King Henry III, who ruled England from 1216 to 1272.

war that had led to Magna Carta had taught John that he could not do exactly as he wished, and it was a lesson that his son King Henry III had learned as well.

However, by the 1250s, Henry was showing signs of following his father's bad example. He brought in foreign favourites to occupy government posts, hired mercenaries to enforce his will and siphoned off government funds for his own purposes. The most contentious, and expensive, of these came in 1253 when Pope Innocent IV offered to make Henry's second son, Edmund, King of Sicily. Henry was naturally eager to gain such a wealthy and prestigious crown for his son. The catch was that the then King of Sicily, Manfred Hohenstaufen, did not recognise the Pope's right to oust him from power and was willing to fight to remain ruler of the island. The resulting war proved to be long and very expensive.

By 1256 the escalating costs of the Sicilian War, added to the underlying concerns that the barons had about King Henry III, led to mutterings against the king. In that year the Welsh Prince Llewellyn II raided into England. Henry raised an army to retaliate, but the expedition was a fiasco plagued by bad organisation, poor supplies and incompetent leadership - all of them Henry's fault.

The next meeting of the Grand Council, the gathering of all nobles, bishops and major landowners, came on 28 April 1258 at Oxford. Simon de Montfort, Earl of Leicester and one of the richest men in England, had spent the previous weeks consulting with his fellow grand nobles. They arrived at the council accompanied by armed men and dressed in armour as if for battle. Henry was taken aback by the demonstration of naked power and demanded to know what the nobles wanted.

De Montfort put forward a document that has become known as the Provisions of Oxford and which was, effectively, England's first constitution. The Provisions stated that the king could enact new laws, raise new taxes or make agreements with other rulers only with the agreement of a Council made up of 24 men, 12 chosen by the Grand Council and 12 chosen by the king. There was to be a new body, the Parliament, composed of representatives elected by the clerics, nobles and knights, which would meet three times a year to supervise and question the Council. And everyone had to abide by the Magna Carta.

As revolutionary measures go, the Provisions of Oxford were very limited. Power was effectively shifted from the king to the leading barons with the lesser noblemen and clerics getting a mere walk on role and the vast mass of the population excluded altogether. Nevertheless in the context of the mid 13th century it was a major constitutional move, one that was unique in Europe where

7

The Provisions of Oxford are presented to King Henry III by Simon de Montfort and his fellow barons in 1258.

the trend was in the other direction with monarchs cementing their powers. Henry was furious, but he signed the document and swore a holy oath to uphold it. The Council was formed, Parliament was summoned. Edmund was ordered home and the Sicilian War was ended. The crisis seemed to be over.

But Henry and his eldest son Edward had no intention of abiding by the

8

In 1263 riots by Londoners supporting the cause of reform forced Queen Eleanor, wife of King Henry III, to flee the city. As she passed under London Bridge in a barge the angry citizens threw rubbish at her, one chamber pot full of filth landing on her head. This insult to royal dignity angered the royalists and had much to do with the savage vengeance that they would later take on the rebel leader, Simon de Montfort, Earl of Leicester.

Provisions of Oxford. Over the following months and years they charmed, flattered and bribed the nobles least committed to the new arrangements. When Henry believed that he had sufficiently undermined the cause of the barons led by de Montfort he sent a message to the new pope, Urban IV, reminding him of Henry's past services and asking to be released from his holy oath. Urban agreed, and Henry lost no time in disbanding the Council and gathering an army of supporters and mercenaries.

De Montfort quickly raised his own army and marched on London. Henry was surprised by de Montfort's quick move and fell back into Sussex to await reinforcements. At Lewes, de Montfort caught up with Henry and inflicted on him a heavy defeat. Henry and Edward were both captured. This time de Montfort took no chances, keeping both king and prince under lock and key. The Provisions

At the Battle of Evesham on 4 August 1265 King Henry III had a narrow escape. Unhorsed and mixed up with the rebel forces he was almost speared by one of his own knights when he was recognised by his eldest son, Edward, who sprang to the rescue.

of Oxford were reintroduced, but this time with freemen being allowed to elect representatives to Parliament for the first time. It was a revolutionary change.

Then Prince Edward escaped captivity, moved with lightning speed to raise a new army. At Evesham he cornered de Montfort with only a few men. De Montfort was defeated and killed, along with most of the men he had with him. However, a great number of his supporters had not been at Evesham. They now began mustering at locations across the kingdom, preparing to continue the fight

Peverel Castle in the north of Derbyshire was disputed between the Earl of Derby and Prince Edward, both of whom had a claim to the castle and its lands, but only one of whom was son of King Henry III. The loss of the castle rankled badly with Derby and had much to do with his decision to rebel.

to force Henry to abide by Magna Carta and the Provisions of Oxford as he had so often promised to do.

The reformist, or rebel, army at Chesterfield was led by Robert de Ferrers, Earl of Derby. This Derby was a prickly and difficult character who inspired great devotion and bitter hatred in almost equal measure. He was, however, one of the richest and most powerful men in England so nobody could afford to ignore him. Born in 1239, Derby was not yet 30 by the time of the Battle of Chesterfield, but he was already suffering from a severe case of gout. This not only hindered his ability to ride or fight, but also worsened his already famously bad temper.

Derby had inherited his title and vast estates at the age of 13. As an orphan he was put into the care of Prince Edward who also took over stewardship of the Derby estates. Three years later in 1257 a rather murky deal took place by which

11

the stewardship of the Derby estates passed to Peter of Savoy who paid Prince Edward in return the hefty sum of 6,000 marks in cash. Peter of Savoy was an Italian nobleman and relative of Eleanor of Provence, queen to Henry III. He had come to England with Eleanor in 1241 and quickly established himself as a foreigner able and willing to do King Henry's dirty work. He amassed great wealth, but a poor reputation. Among his acquisitions was land between Strand and the Thames in London where he built the Savoy Palace, on the site of which now stands the Savoy Hotel. Exactly what the terms of the deal were we do not know, but we do know that young Derby greatly resented them. He later claimed that he had been robbed of much of his birthright, so it is reasonable to assume that either Edward or Peter, or both, looted his estates and drained them of wealth.

Chesterfield from the north. The twisted church spire can be clearly seen, marking the northeastern corner of the old town.

In 1260 Derby came of age and took possession of his lands. In that first year he derived an income of £1,500 in rents and other payments. His lands were concentrated in the northern midlands. He owned all Lancashire between the Mersey and the Ribble, most of southern Derbyshire and estates in Nottinghamshire and Staffordshire, including the powerful Chartley Castle.

When de Montfort first raised an army, Derby was quick to declare his allegiance to the rebel cause. He did not, however, march to join de Montfort. Instead he raised a sizeable force with which he attacked and seized castles and lands belonging to Prince Edward. The suspicion must be, therefore, that Derby was more interested in paying off his old scores with Edward than with helping de Montfort. Among the properties Derby grabbed at this time were the castles of Grosmont, Skenfrith and Whitecastle in south Wales, estates in Worcestershire, Bolsover Castle, Horston Castle, Tickhill Castle and finally Peverel Castle in northern Derbyshire. This last was a particularly sore spot for Derby.

The castle had come into the Derby family by way of Margaret Peverel, great great grandmother of Derby. However, the castle and its lands had only ever been in the stewardship of the Derbys, not owned by them, due to vagaries of medieval

The arms of Robert Ferrers, Earl of Derby, in the centre the red and yellow banded waves of the Earldom of Derby surrounded by the black horseshoes on white of the Ferrers family. They include the sort of pun beloved by the medieval mind. The horseshoes are a pun on the surname "Ferrers", that being close to the Norman-French word for horseshoes, even though the word derived from Ferriers, the birthplace of the first Earl of Derby.

13

land law. King Henry III had taken the unusual step of availing himself of the right to terminate that stewardship. Peverel Castle and its lands had then been passed to Prince Edward during the time when Edward was looking after the Derby estates. At some point around 1263 Edward and Derby had quarrelled over Peverel Castle. The monk Robert of Gloucester who was writing a chronicle at this time recorded "Of no man was Lord Edward more afraid than of Lord Derby." Clearly de Montfort's rising was a useful pretext for Derby to get back at Edward.

That Simon de Montfort did not trust Derby is shown by events in January 1265. When Derby went to London to attend the Parliament summoned by de Montfort. When he arrived, Derby found himself accused of stealing royal lands, which he undoubtedly had done, and thrown into the Tower of London to await trial. He was still there when de Montfort was defeated and killed at Evesham in August 1265.

When King Henry III arrived in London one of his first tasks was to do a deal with Derby. Derby had a lot of support in the Midlands and, as a former rebel, could be used to bring other rebels back to loyalty to the crown. In return for a small fine and a promise to return Prince Edward's properties, Derby was released and told to return to his estates.

Derby left London and hurried north, heading for his mighty Duffield Castle in southern Derbyshire. Once there Derby made contact with Sir Baldwin de Wake, lord of Chesterfield, and John d'Ayville. These two noblemen had remained loyal to de Montfort throughout, but had not been at Evesham for the fatal battle. They were uncertain what fate King Henry had in store for them and were still in arms. Wake soon joined Derby at Duffield with a small force. d'Ayville was in Yorkshire with a larger force of armed men. He sent word that he would come to Duffield by way of Chesterfield.

However, at Tutbury Castle was a sizeable royal army led by Henry of Almain, nephew of King Henry. Hearing that d'Ayville was on the move, Henry marched north, going by way of Ashbourne to avoid Duffield Castle and its rebels. His aim was to intercept d'Ayville before he reached Duffield and if at all possible ambush him on the road. Derby in turn learned that Henry of Almain was marching north and guessed his intentions. He himself set off north with Wake and made for Chesterfield, of which Wake was lord and where they could count on a warm welcome.

The rival armies were by now all on the march and converging on Chesterfield. The stage was set for the battle.

14

CHAPTER 2
LEADERS AT CHESTERFIELD

The Battle of Chesterfield was a complex battle, made no more straightforward by the fact that there were four armies and four commanders involved.

Of the four commanders at the Battle of Chesterfield more is known of Robert de Ferrers, 6th Earl of Derby than of the others. The mighty Ferrers family originated with Walkeline de Ferrers the lord of the manor at Ferrières-Saint-Hilaire, a small village in Normandy. Walkeline died in about 1040 leaving three sons. Two of these, William and Henry joined Duke of William of Normandy in his invasion of England in 1066. William was killed in the Battle of Hastings, but Henry survived. He was given extensive lands in the northern Midlands, on which he built Tutbury and Duffield Castles. Henry's son Robert was given the title Earl of Derby in 1138, passing that prestigious title on to his son Robert. By a series of judicious marriages, the Ferrers increased their lands and wealth even more until by the time Robert became the 6th Earl they were one of the richest ten families in the kingdom.

By the time he set off for Chesterfield, Derby had acquired a great deal of experience of military campaigning, but almost no experience of any actual fighting. His marches in 1264 to seize lands and properties from Prince Edward had seen him take a small army from Derbyshire to south Wales, then back again through Worcestershire and Staffordshire. This represents a round distance of well over 300 miles. Given that medieval armies usually struggled to make more than 12 miles a day except in an emergency that is some 25 days of marching. Add in the delays caused by the need to seize, garrison and organise the lands and castles that Derby got hold of, and it is likely that Derby and his army were on the move for some six weeks or more. Even allowing for the fact that Derby probably had a fairly small force with him this still represents a considerable achievement in terms of supply and navigational logistics.

Derby could clearly lead men on campaign. This was no real surprise. Leading

15

armies and fighting in battle was a standard part of the upbringing of a nobleman. He will from childhood have been practising with sword, lance and mace. He would have trained to ride a horse down cliffs, across rivers swollen by flood and into the noise and bustle of battle. He would have studied the less exciting but no less important business of keeping men supplied with food, shoes and coats when on campaign. But though Derby had learned all these things, and had marched on campaign, he had never actually been to war. Neither, for that matter, had his father. William de Ferrers, 5th Earl of Derby, had been recognised as a clever man and able administrator, but he had been crippled almost from birth. Unable to ride a horse, let alone charge one into battle, the 5th Earl had to travel in a cart or litter. So, Derby had seen no real fighting and he was an untested commander.

Baldwin de Wake, lord of Chesterfield, is not so well recorded as Derby. The

A relief of Simon de Montfort, Earl of Leicester, attached to the modern battle monument at Lewes in Sussex, the scene of his greatest victory. Henry of Almain had become a sworn enemy of de Montfort and all he stood for by 1266, having jeered at de Montfort's corpse at Evesham.

Wakes came from the lower ranks of the nobility in the county of Yorkshire. He was born in about 1238, making him in his late 20s at the time of the Battle of Chesterfield. From his father Hugh he inherited the Lordship of Bourne along with lands in Yorkshire. His mother was Ela Beauchamp, daughter of the wealthy William de Beauchamp who gave his daughter two manors in Lincolnshire that then passed to Baldwin.

Unlike Derby, Wake came from a famous fighting family. His father Hugh had died fighting the Moslems on Crusade. His grandfather, another Baldwin, had fought extensively for King John against the French, and then against King John in the campaigns that led to the signing of Magna Carta. The Wake family therefore had a track record of opposing royal power as well as of being active fighters. Wake himself had fought at the Siege of Northampton in 1264 and at the Siege of Kenilworth in 1265. He was made Lord of Chesterfield by de Montfort, who presumably wanted that key fortified town in the hands of a supporter. He missed the Battles of Lewes and Evesham and by the spring of 1266 was back on his estates in Yorkshire.

Wake seems to have reached some sort of an agreement with King Henry after Evesham, but the details of this have not survived. Presumably he was worried that Henry might not respect the agreement, or perhaps he hoped that a new rebellion would secure a better form of peace than the triumphant Henry and Edward had imposed after Evesham. Whatever his motives, Wake came to Duffield Castle with a small force in April 1266 to join the uprising being organised by Derby.

Sir John d'Ayville is even less well known. He was considerably older than either Wake or Derby, being in his 50s, or perhaps even his 60s. He owned Hode, or Hood, Castle near High Kilburn. Like the Wakes, the d'Ayvilles had a history of rebellion. John's father, another Sir John, had been in the forces that forced the Magna Carta on King John. It was during the turbulent years running up to Magna Carta that the elder Sir John had converted his manor house at Hode into a small castle. There seems to have been some dispute as to whether the d'Ayville's had ever got formal permission to build this castle, but despite objections from Henry III early in his reign the castle remained standing. It was, however, small as were the d'Ayville estates. They seem to have amounted to little more than half a dozen manors. Nothing is known of d'Ayville's military career before Chesterfield, though on the day of battle he proved to be the most competent of the three rebels so perhaps he had seen some real fighting.

The royalist commander, Henry of Almain, was the most prestigious of the men who fought at Chesterfield. Born in 1235 he was 29 on the day of battle, but was little more experienced at warfare than was Derby. Henry was the son of Richard, 1st Earl of Cornwall, the younger brother of King Henry III. Richard was given vast estates that made him, after the king, the richest man in England. He went on Crusade in 1239 where he gained a great reputation for both fighting and for humanity - his most famous act being to negotiate a truce in the midst of a battle to allow for the wounded to be treated and the dead buried. In 1256 Richard was elected King of Germany by the German nobles, but he was never able to make a reality of his regime given the opposition of some powerful German nobles. When the de Montfort rebellion began Richard came back to England to fight on the side of his brother.

Young Henry, however, was never quite so certain in his loyalties. His mother Isabel was a daughter of the great nobleman William Marshal who had been one of the leaders of the Magna Carta rebellion. He was also related by marriage to the Montfort family. When the war broke out Henry at first avoided taking sides and attempted to stay on friendly terms with both King Henry and de Montfort. When this proved impossible to maintain he opted to support the king. He did not take part in the Battle of Lewes but instead embarked on a series of minor campaigns securing castles and towns for his royal uncle. There does not seem to have been any actual fighting on these campaigns. He was at Evesham, but he held no command position and his role seems to have been restricted to gloating over the corpse of Simon de Montfort once the fighting was over.

The size of the armies engaged at Chesterfield is not know for certain. Medieval chroniclers were never very accurate in recording the size of armies, being always rather more interested in the deeds and fates of the famous men involved. They usually content themselves with describing armies as "large", "enormous" or "small". When they do hazard a guess at the size of armies, contemporary writers almost certainly over estimate. One chronicler said that at the Battle of Lewes de Montfort had 60,000 men though it seems certain that he had less than 10,000.

It is impossible to know for certain how many men were fighting at Chesterfield, but it would seem reasonable to suppose that Henry of Almain had perhaps 1,000 fighting men, plus the usual supernumeraries, while the rebels had slighter fewer. Both sides seem to have been short on knights and mounted men at arms, a fact which controlled the scope and pattern of the fighting.

CHAPTER 3
MEN, WEAPONS AND TACTICS

At the time the Battle of Chesterfield was fought, Europe was still very much a feudal society. The heart of the feudal society was an economic-military deal in which a king or nobleman granted a temporary lease on land to another man in return for service. The economic underpinning of the entire system was at the very bottom of the social pyramid where land was given to peasants in return for a set number of days labour in the landlord's fields in they course of the year. The freed the landlord from the need to do any actual work himself and allowed him to concentrate on other tasks instead.

Some land holders were abbeys or cathedrals or monasteries who contributed to society in other ways, but the vast majority were laymen and their task was to fight. It is with them that we are concerned here.

Although there were variations, land was usually parcelled out in what were known as "knight's fees", that is the amount of land needed to generate income to support a knight and allow him to be able to afford a warhorse, a riding horse and the arms, armour and supplies that he needed to go to war.

Each knight had to serve for a set number of days each year in return for his fee. This was usually between 40 and 60 days and though the lord could ask the knight to serve for longer the knight could refuse and, if he agreed, expected to be paid. It also seems to have been the case that while the knight was expected to feed himself and suffer the cost of any lost or damaged equipment during his first 40 or 60 days of service, once he was being paid the lord had to keep him supplied and replace anything that got or damaged - including the horse.

War horses were extremely expensive animals at this date costing perhaps five or six times as much as a riding horse. The cost was not so much due to the type of horse, for war horses were only slightly larger than riding horses, but to the training. A war horse had to have the stamina to go on long marches, often with only sparse or poor quality fodder. And once into battle, the war horse had to remain calm and obedient without being timid or scared. Moreover it was expected to be able to carry out a wide range of moves unknown to other horses. It had to rear up and stomp on men on command, kick backwards at other horses or turn around in its own length. Only a minority of horses were able to do these things, and those that could took years to train. No wonder a horse was a knight's most valued piece of equipment.

Some knights did not go on campaign, but were instead allocated to castle guard duty. This had the advantage of being carried out close to home, but usually lasted longer with 3 months being the average. Castle guard duty did not always involve manning a castle, it might refer to commanding a town militia to guard a town or other garrison tasks. It has been conjectured that older knights or those suffering long term wounds stood castle guard, but this is by no means certain.

Not all knight's fees were held by knights. Some fees were handed to two sergeants instead of a single knight. A sergeant at this date was a mounted soldier who lacked the heavy armour and well trained war horse of a knight. This meant he was not as much use in a battle, but he was invaluable on campaign. To sergeants fell the tasks of patrols, skirmishing, riding ahead to seize bridges, securing food supplies and grabbing hapless peasants to question them about enemy troop movements.

Sergeants would usually invest in a metal helmet, but their body armour tended to be of boiled leather or gambeson, a type of heavy quilted fabric firmly stuffed with wool or old cloth.

Some knight's fees were divided in other ways, providing four infantrymen, for example.

Just as not all knight's fees provided knights to the army, not all of them took the form of land. A knight's fee might be an annual cash payment, or perhaps the right to levy import or export duties at a small port. Almost anything in the gift of a king or lord might comprise a knight's fee. In theory none of these fees were hereditary, but by the 13th century in practice they were. All a son and heir had to do was pay a sum to the lord and he inherited his father's lands, and his duties.

It is thought that in the 13th century England was divided into about 7,000 knight's fees of land with another 1,000 or 1,500 knight's fees taking the form of non-land fees.

Of course, no king would divide all his lands up into individual knight's fees and distribute them himself. In the days before writing was a common skill and government bureaucracy was non-existent such a system would not work. Instead a ruler tended to hand large numbers of knight's fees to great nobles, who then

This figure of a heavily armoured knight is based on the funerary monument of Sir Geoffrey de Magnaville, buried in the early 13th century. A contemporary stained glass window of Simon de Montfort at Chartres, France, shows him in almost identical kit. This figure wears an iron helmet padded with leather over a mail coif. This type of helmet first appeared about 1140 and remained very common through to around 1240, though by 1266 they were becoming a bit old fashioned. The heraldic charge on his shield is repeated on the side of the helmet. The mail hauberk reaches to his knees and is slit front and back to allow him to sit astride his horse. His mail leggings reach from above the knee to the toes. His right arm would have been covered in mail to the wrist, with a mail gauntlet protecting his hand and fingers. The left arm, protected by the shield, lacked mail. The shield is attached to a strap to save it being dropped. His lance is not shown, but his long sword hangs from his belt.

parcelled them out to lesser nobles who in turn gave them to individual knights, sergeants and so forth.

This form of feudalism was the system that the Normans imported to England when they conquered the kingdom in 1066. However, in England there were three key factors not found on the continent that the Normans kept and which made England unique. First was the concept that many people paid a cash sum instead of rendering service. For military duties this payment was known as "scutage", meaning "shield money" and equated to the sum needed to pay a mercenary to do the duty instead. By the 13th century it is thought that the majority of knight's fees in England paid scutage instead of performing service.

The second feature was that every able bodied freeman (that is not slaves or serfs) aged between 16 and 60 had to turn out armed and ready for local defence. This obligation was traditionally limited to the shire where the person lived and lasted only as long as an enemy army was in the shire. This formed the basis of the local militias of England. In the mid-13th century the development of these was still in flux but it seems that already a community would band together to afford the equipment of a man chosen, or volunteering, to go to war. The militiamen would later become well-trained and valuable part-time soldiers, but in the 1260s most were still amateurs able only to perform second rank duties.

The third key feature of military service in England was that every man right down the chain of feudal obligations even down to the lowest serf or slave owed allegiance and loyalty to the king. The intermediate nobles and knights were merely agents of the king. On the continent each person owed allegiance only to their immediate superior, so if a nobleman rebelled against his king all his feudal adherents were obliged to join the rebellion.

In England the loyalty to the king tended to put a brake on rebellions and made civil wars much less frequent and less widespread than on the continent. When Simon de Montfort led his uprising he claimed that he was raising troops on behalf of the king in order to rescue him from the influence of foreign and wicked advisers. It was not true, of course, but it was a necessary legal fiction to persuade men to join his rebellion.

The size of units raised under the feudal system varied enormously. One nobleman might bring two knights, four sergeants and half a dozen infantrymen with him to war, others would have several hundred of each. Such units served under their feudal superior and often resented being sent off on detached duty. It was generally easier for a commander to send off a junior nobleman with a small retinue to do a task than to ask a great magnate to divide his force. All of which made command structure on the battlefield somewhat complex.

The various ranks of noblemen expected to be treated with the honour due their rank, irrespective of how many men they commanded or how experienced they were at war. Thus a king had to give commands to an earl before a baron, and to a baron before a knight. A commander might find himself in the awkward position of having to give orders to a young, untried earl while an experienced baron with a large contingent hung about in the background. In most instances tact and understanding could get around such issues, but not always.

Mention has been made of mercenaries. This term today has negative connotations, but in the 13th century being a mercenary was an honourable and honest profession that attracted men from all levels of society. Even the great nobles might spend time as a mercenary before inheriting their estates and the responsibilities that went with them.

The figure on which this man is based is described as a Londoner in the manuscript where he appears, but he is typical of the sort of man who would be recruited by any medieval army in large numbers. He is equipped with a metal helmet, padded inside with wool and leather and with a kite-shaped shield that covers him from shoulder to knee. His main weapon is a short thrusting spear and he would have had a heavy knife or small hatchet tucked into his belt as a reserve weapon. In action these men formed up shoulder to shoulder with their shields overlapping to form a solid wall of shields facing the enemy. Spears were usually held overarm and thrust forward and down over the shield at the enemy. Whether a unit of such men would be able to carry out any of the more sophisticated battle tactics of this period would depend on their level of training. As a rule town militia were better trained than rural militia, but not so good as mercenaries.

Mercenaries served for cash payments. Although those sums were usually expressed in daily terms - 24 pennies for a knight, 12 pennies for a sergeant and two pennies for a foot soldier were typical - contracts were usually negotiated for a fixed term of months. At this date there were no permanent mercenary bands or armies as would come later, but there were famous mercenary captains who knew where and how to recruit surprisingly large numbers of men at short notice. Mercenaries serving in England tended to be German, French or Breton. They were armed and equipped in much the same way as English fighting men. Elsewhere in Europe there were specialised troops skilled at certain types of fighting - such as the Basque mercenaries adept at mountain warfare - but they seem to have been absent from England.

Mercenaries were much better disciplined, better trained and better equipped than a feudal army. As a result they were popular with kings, but they were

This figure is based on a French manuscript of about 1280 that shows an English mercenary. This figure is wearing the sort of equipment to which town and county militia aspired, but rarely achieved. His helmet is of iron, padded inside with a thick leather lining stuffed with wool. The mail hauberk has a coif under the helmet and reaches to the thighs and elbows. Over the hauberk he wears a sleeveless tunic made of thick leather on to which have been sewn overlapping scales made from horn. The lower legs and arms are bare of armour. His triangular shield is about 30 inches tall and 24 inches wide and is made of thin, overlapping sheets of wood faced with boiled leather stretched to fit and then left to harden. The shield would have been painted with the heraldic device of the mercenary's employer, or that of the town or county from which the militia came. His main weapon is a 10 foot long thrusting spear, with a short sword for back up.

expensive and because they demanded payment in cash in a society where most taxes and business deals were done in kind even rich men could not always pay them. Mercenaries were, in theory, organised in units of 10 and 100 men, with larger mercenary armies being composed of units of 100.

The reputation of medieval warfare has suffered in recent years. It is often supposed that medieval battles were little more than disorganised scrummages of murderous violence carried out by ignorant men possessed of little more than brute force and big swords. This was very far from being the case. Medieval warfare had a surprisingly complex range of tactics and manoeuvres on which a commander could call. Admittedly only the well trained mercenaries could be relied upon to carry this out reliably and with precision, the less professional feudal soldiers might attempt such manoeuvres but in the heat of battle with enemies pressing in they could not always be relied upon to do so successfully.

The basic infantry tactic was the shield wall. This was composed of several ranks of men, usually 8 or so deep, standing shoulder to shoulder. They presented their overlapping shields to the enemy to form a solid wall of shields - hence the name of the formation. Good men could move about the battlefield at a jog and still maintain formation, though most preferred to walk and even then might have to stop every now and then to get back into shape.

Most infantrymen came armed with a spear, which was used to stab at the enemy over the top of a shield wall, but others came to war with axes, swords or bows. There seems to have been little effort made to separate out these men. They all formed up in the shield wall as a mixed mass of different weaponry, presumably with all the men from one area choosing to stand together.

The basic cavalry tactic was the charge, delivered by two or three ranks of horsemen riding knee to knee. Each rank was 20 or so yards behind the one in front so that if a horse fell those behind stood a chance of jumping over it or veering out the way before they too were brought down. A charge of armoured knights delivered at the right time was devastating. Choosing when to launch this charge was perhaps the most important decision a 13th century commander had to make. Well formed infantry could withstand a charge for no horse will gallop straight into a solid object - including a wall of men. But even the slightest disorder would cause a formation to crack under the impact of a charge. Poorly trained infantry would often simply run away in the face of a charge of knights.

And once an army was fragmented and fleeing a commander would find it very difficult indeed to restore order and discipline.

Infantry delivering a pig snout attack. The triangle of men pushed forward would be the most experienced and toughest in the formation. Their task was to punch a hole in the enemy shield wall, then move forward allowing the rest of the formation to advance and split the enemy infantry into two pieces ready to be cut to pieces.

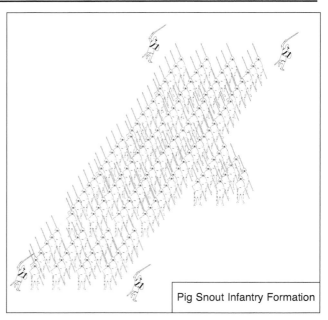

Pig Snout Infantry Formation

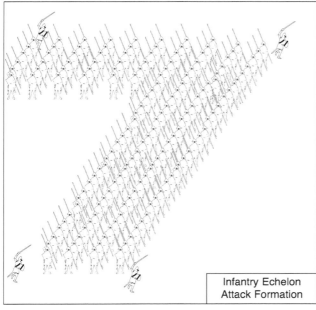

Infantry Echelon Attack Formation

Infantry attacking with weight on the flank. This required great discipline. The attack was delivered at the trot, coming to a halt once contact was made with the opposing shield wall. The extra men on the left flank would then push forward in a packed formation akin to a modern rugby scrum in an effort to disrupt the enemy line and begin a retreat that could be turned in to a rout.

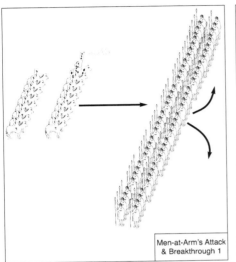

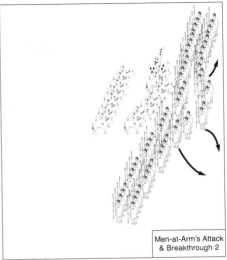

Men-at-Arm's Attack & Breakthrough 1

Men-at-Arm's Attack & Breakthrough 2

A sequence of diagrams showing armoured cavalry breaking a formation of poorly trained infantry. 1 - The cavalry charge, some infantry begin to flee. 2 - The cavalry make contact, more infantry flee while others are killed. 3 - The cavalry break through as the infantry formation breaks up. 4 - The pursuit begins with the cavalry able to kill the fleeing infantry with ease.

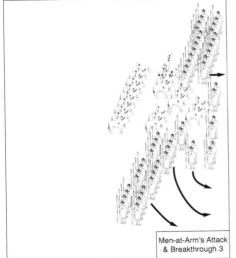

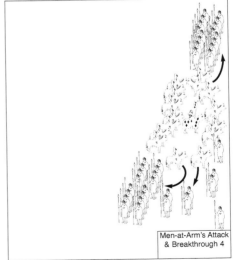

Men-at-Arm's Attack & Breakthrough 3

Men-at-Arm's Attack & Breakthrough 4

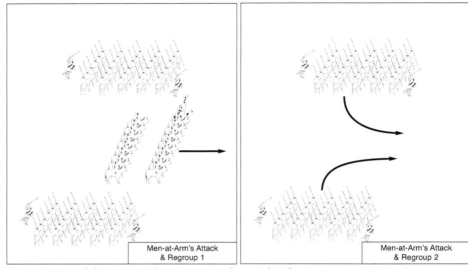

A sequence of diagrams showing cavalry and infantry co-operating in an attack. 1 - The infantry part to allow the cavalry through. 2 - While the cavalry deliver their attack the infantry form a defensive shield wall. 3 - When the depleted cavalry return defeated they take cover behind the infantry. 4 - The army adopts a defensive stance while the commander decides what to do next.

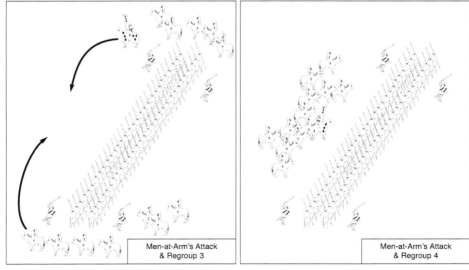

Chapter 5
The Battle of Chesterfield

A t the time of the battle, Chesterfield was a small market town - a borough in the language of the time. Although we have no contemporary descriptions of the time, it is possible to reconstruct a fair image of what the town was like from archaeological remains and the written references that have survived.

The town had become a borough in 1204, receiving a charter from King John. Gaining a charter was a crucial step for a town from many points of view. From an economic aspect the charter could be relied upon to give the town an edge

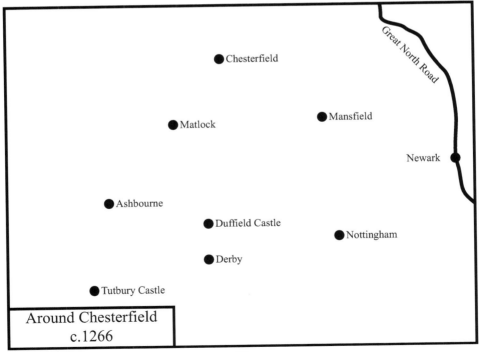

Around Chesterfield
c.1266

over nearby settlements. Although the terms varied, a borough was allowed to hold a regular market, fair or both. These brought great numbers of traders and customers to the town. Not only did this great influx of people spend money in taverns and shops, but the traders had to rent the stalls from the town authorities while they might also have to pay a percentage of their income to the town as well. Chesterfield gained a market from its charter, making it the undisputed centre of trade for the surrounding countryside.

Socially a charter also bestowed important benefits on a town. Again the details varied, but a chartered borough was generally free of interference in its affairs by local nobles, churchmen or clerics. Chesterfield was a Free Borough, meaning that the town ran its own affairs, subject only to the jurisdiction of the king and his officers, primarily the county sheriff. The wealthier freemen of the town elected the mayor and other officials who ran the town's administration, organised the paving of streets, the disposal of waste and other matters.

Of particular relevance to the battle fought here in 1266 was the fact that

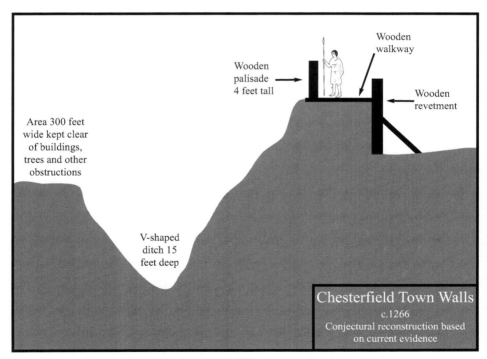

Area 300 feet wide kept clear of buildings, trees and other obstructions

Wooden palisade 4 feet tall

Wooden walkway

Wooden revetment

V-shaped ditch 15 feet deep

Chesterfield Town Walls
c.1266
Conjectural reconstruction based on current evidence

The coat of arms of Chesterfield shows as its crest a ram, the traditional symbol of Derbyshire, standing atop a mural crown, or circlet made of stone or brick. This was traditionally given only to towns with defensive walls.

boroughs were expected to have town walls. These performed a variety of purposes. They kept wild animals out and domestic animals in. They were also essential to the smooth running of the market. Traders could not enter or leave except through a fixed number of gates, so there was no chance that they would evade paying their dues. They were also useful for maintaining law and order as the gates could be closed while a miscreant was pursued or if a gang of outlaws was in the area.

From the point of view of the king, one of the key advantages of making a town a borough was that he thereby gained a fortified place, the inhabitants of which were loyal to him instead of to some local noble. If there were any civil unrest, and King John had suffered more than his fair share of that, the king could send troops to garrison a town knowing that it had defences and that it could serve as a base for operations in the area.

Boroughs were usually assessed for the militia, and some kept a town guard composed of a small number of men permanently on duty. In the event of invasion or disturbance, the inhabitants of local villages could pour into the borough to shelter behind its walls until the danger had passed.

The nature of the town walls at Chesterfield has long been a matter of controversy. Not only are there no town walls today, but there is no trace of them in Tudor or Stuart times when most towns were dismantling their medieval fortifications. However, the town's coat of arms feature a mural crown, a crown around the helmet on top of the coat of arms that is composed of stones. This device was traditionally restricted to towns with walls, though there were exceptions.

Archeological digs in Chesterfield have shown that the hill crowned by the Church of St Mary and All Saints was formerly occupied by an iron age village and a Roman army fort. The site was naturally easy to defend, with rivers on two sides and fairly steep slopes leading up to the summit. The southern edge of the Roman fort was south of Church Lane and its eastern edge along what is now Station Road. The northern and western sides of the fort are unclear, but it probably covered about 7 acres.

The medieval town occupied much the same area as the Roman fort. What appears to have been the medieval ditch outside the walls has been found in Station Road. This was a wide, V-shaped ditch about 15 feet deep. Broken pottery shows that it was filled in during the later 15th century. If this ditch is what remains of the medieval town walls then nothing of any actual wall has survived. However, comparison with similar structures elsewhere shows what the town walls would have been like in 1266.

The earth excavated from the ditch would have been piled up behind the ditch to form a mound of earth. This served to increase the vertical distance from the bottom of the ditch back up to the ground surface. The mound would have been constained within wooden revetments to keep it in place. On top of the mound would have been placed a wooden pallisade around four feet tall. The actual top of the mound may have been left as bare earth, or may have had a wooden walkway laid on top of it. The defenders of the town would have stood on the walkway and sheltered behind the pallisade when fighting any attackers. The ground immediately outside the ditch would have been cleared of trees, bushes and buildings to a distance of around 300 feet or so. This was so that no attackers could creep up to the walls unobserved.

By the standards of the mid-13th century, these walls were obsolete and next to useless. Techniques to overcome earth and timber defences were well known, so even a mediocre commander of a small army could expect to be inside Chesterfield within a day or two. Given that the town guard was likely to be as poorly put together as the town walls it may not have taken even that long. Most towns of any size had stone walls by this date, usually with towers and sophisticated gatehouses. Presumably the town walls of Chesterfield were more for monitoring those attending the market than for any real attempt at defence.

The first of the armies to arrive in Chesterfield was the combined force of Derby and Wake. They marched into the town on 15 May, probably around the middle of the day. No doubt the commanders busied themselves finding billets

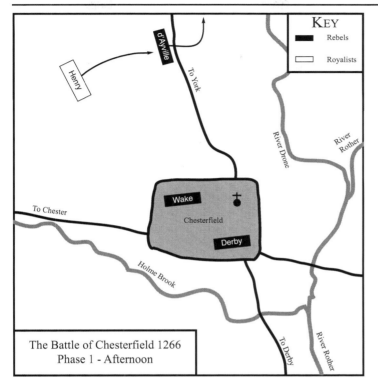

KEY

Rebels

Royalists

The Battle of Chesterfield 1266
Phase 1 - Afternoon

The Battle of Chesterfield began some time in the afternoon of 15 May 1266 when the advancing rebels of Sir John d'Aynville were ambushed north of the town by the royalists led by Henry of Almain.

for their men, posting lookouts and perhaps sending out patrols to look for d'Ayville. Derby himself was undergoing one of his periodic attacks of gout. At some point in the afternoon he went off to look for a doctor to give him some relief from his pain.

The precise chronology of what happened next is not easy to reconstruct from the sparse accounts that have survived. The reading that makes perhaps the most sense has d'Ayville advancing toward Chesterfield on the road from York and the north, west of the Rother. He and his men must have been approaching Chesterfield in the late afternoon. Some distance from Chesterfield, and apparently out of sight of Derby and Wake's lookouts on the town walls, d'Ayville was attacked by Henry of Almain's force.

The initial attack was carried out by mounted knights, charging out of cover towards the rebel force that was strung out along the road. D'Ayville immediately realised the seriousness of his situation. If Henry's charging, armoured horsemen

33

got among his infantry before they had formed up the result would be a massacre. Fortunately d'Ayville had suspected that Henry's force might not be far off and had ordered his men to march in armour, as he himself was doing. Gathering the few mounted knights that he had with him, d'Ayville put spurs to his horse and charged toward the advancing royalists.

At the very first clash, d'Ayville went down. He was knocked from his horse by the lance wielded by Sir Gilbert Hansard, one of the royalist knights. Capturing an enemy nobleman, and even more so the enemy commander, was an act of great prestige. It could also be extremely profitable for even if the enemy was not able to pay much ransom he would command a high price from his enemies. The fall of d'Ayville thus entirely unhinged the royalist attack. Instead of pushing on to slaughter the unprepared infantry, the royalists drew rein in the hope of capturing d'Ayville. It proved to be a mistake.

D'Ayville's own knights were just as determined to get their commander away safely as were the royalists to capture him. A savage fight developed around the unhorsed elderly knight, but it was the rebels who had the best of it. They managed to drag d'Ayville from the scrimmage and get him back to the safety of his infantry, now fully formed up and ready to fight.

It would seem that d'Ayville had either been put out of action or was disconcerted by the size and aggressiveness of the royalists. Whether by orders of d'Ayville or his subordinates if he were out of action, the rebel army began moving back to the north and away from Chesterfield.

At this point Henry of Almain had a choice. He could either pursue d'Ayville to scatter his forces and ensure that they could not regroup, or he could turn south to tackle Derby and Wake in Chesterfield. We cannot now know why Henry made the decision he did, but it is not too difficult to guess at the factors that weighed on his mind.

Chasing an already defeated enemy was tempting. It would undoubtedly be better to destroy d'Ayville's small force than allow it to escape and reform. On the other hand, D'Ayville for all his valour and experience was relatively unimportant. He was a minor rural knight whose castle was small and weak, in reality not much more than a fortified manor house. Even if he managed to get back home without running into another royalist force, d'Ayville could be easily dealt with later.

The Earl of Derby, on the other hand, was a much more dangerous figure. He may have lacked d'Ayville's skill and experience, but he was enormously wealthy, very well connected and ranked right at the top of England's nobility. The capture or death of Derby was of paramount importance if King Henry III was to sit secure on this throne. Not only that, but in Chesterfield Derby was vulnerable. The town walls were weak and could be easily overcome. But if Derby were to be allowed to return to Duffield Castle he would be much more secure. Duffield was not especially large, but it was fully up to date with massive stone walls, high towers and a host of cunning contrived defensive measures.

It is easy to see why Henry decided to leave d'Ayville alone and go for Derby

A modern re-enactor dressed as an archer. At this date English armies had not yet perfected the arrowstorm tactic that would win them great victories against the French at Crecy, Agincourt and elsewhere. The use of bows was instead dissipated along the line which lessened their impact. They were, nevertheless, a significant weapon on the field of battle. With thanks to the Medieval Combat Society.

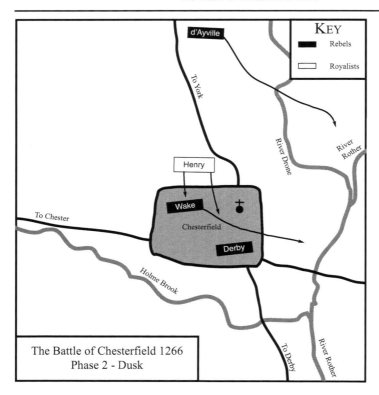

The Battle of Chesterfield 1266
Phase 2 - Dusk

As dusk began to fall, Henry of Almain led the royalist forces in a surprise attack on Chesterfield town, where the Earl of Derby and Sir Baldwin de Wake were resting with their men. Unknown to Henry, however, the rebel force led by d'Aynville had not retreated north but was moving south to support Derby.

instead. He accordingly turned south and perhaps around dusk launched an assault on Chesterfield, presumably on its northern wall.

The attack by Henry and his men took the rebels inside Chesterfield entirely by surprise. It is said that many of the men were in bed when the alarm was sounded. Quite how this managed to happen is not entirely clear. Derby and Wake may not have seen much in the way of actual fighting, but they were both well trained military commanders who had been on campaign. They knew that Henry of Almain was on the march and somewhere in the area, and yet they allowed themselves to be taken entirely by surprise. Standard procedure at the time would have been to close the town gates, post sentries on the walls and, perhaps, send out patrols. Derby and Wake seem to have done none of these things - or if they did their men did not carry out their orders.

It might be possible to excuse Derby. He was very ill with a painful attack of gout and had gone off to find a doctor, but Wake was perfectly fit and well. On

The Old Post House Restaurant in Holywell Street, Chesterfield. In 1266 this would have been just outside the northern walls of the town. It was past here that the royalists led by Henry of Almain led their surprise dusk attack on the town and its rebel garrison.

the other hand the success of Henry's attack may have had more to do with his skill than with mistakes by Wake. Wake was, after all, expecting d'Ayville to approach from the north at any moment. Perhaps the sentries mistook Henry's men for those of d'Ayville.

Whatever the reasons, the results were clear. Many of the rebels did not have time to get into their armour and those that did were completely disorganised and hopelessly muddled. In the narrow streets of Chesterfield and the gathering gloom of dusk there was no chance of restoring order. Sir Baldwin de Wake led the disorganised rout of the rebel forces.

Which way they went is unclear, but the layout of the land suggests that going south or east would be most likely. The rout continued for some time. Inside Chesterfield, Henry of Almain was searching for the rebel leaders. Given the apparent chaos this was no easy task. The streets were filled with armed men, tearing about in different directions or lying dead or wounded on the cobbles.

This was in an age before uniforms, so working out who was on which side was not always easy. Identifying a leader from a follower was rather easier, as the rank and file soldiers would have had lower quality arms and armour. The really important men, such as Derby, would have worn jewellery and fine fabrics that would have instantly picked them out from the crowd. On the other hand this was before the days of photographs and celebrity magazines. The only people who could recognise the Earl of Derby for certain were those who had already met him. And in narrow streets, gathering dusk and when an enemy could attack at any moment it was no easy task to sort out who was who.

Within an hour or so, Henry and his men had the town of Chesterfield secured. The only rebels left within the town walls, they believed, were dead or were prisoners. It slowly became clear to Henry that he had failed to capture any of the leading rebels. This will have come as a disappointment, but was no great blow. The enemy had been caught before they managed to join forces and had been defeated soundly - or so it seemed.

Henry's next task was to care for his wounded men and secure the town. He sent for the mayor and other leading dignitaries. Where they met him and what they discussed is not recorded, but presumably it was a meeting dominated by the practicalities of food, water, medical care and the like.

If Henry of Almain did not know where the Earl of Derby was, neither did his own men. Sir Baldwin de Wake had managed to rally most of his men a mile or so from the town. Before long he was joined by d'Ayville and the survivors of his force. The experienced d'Ayville had not retreated north at all, but had come south in the darkness in an attempt to make contact with Derby and find out what the true situation was. This made him a brave man as well as a resolute commander.

Wake and d'Ayville held a rapid discussion. They still had most of their men, and those of Derby, to hand. They had been beaten and put to flight but the retreat from Chesterfield was not such a rout as had been supposed. Most of the men

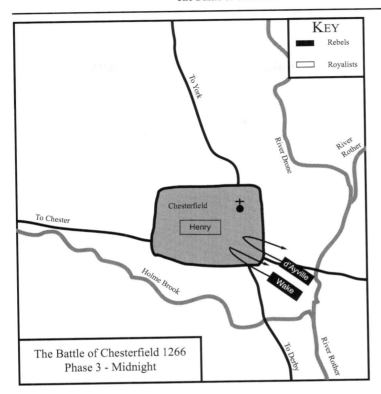

KEY

Rebels

Royalists

To York

River Drone

River Rother

Chesterfield

Henry

To Chester

Holme Brook

d'Ayville

Wake

To Derby

River Rother

The Battle of Chesterfield 1266
Phase 3 - Midnight

The final act in the Battle of Chesterfield came around midnight when the rebels led by Wake and d'Aynville made a final assault on Chesterfield. They reached the market place and got close to the church, but were then driven off by the royalists of Henry of Almain.

were still present, most of those had at least some weapons or armour. What was missing was the Earl of Derby.

The last Wake had seen of Derby was in the late afternoon when he declared he was off to find a doctor to look at his gout. He had not been seen since, and was not in the fields outside Chesterfield with his men. Presumably he had either been killed or captured in the fighting, or was still at liberty inside Chesterfield somewhere.

Wake and d'Ayville's options were limited. They could flee back to their own lands, but that would be to abandon the rebellion and would mean seeking peace terms from King Henry III. Henry had proven himslef to be a bad-tempered, stubborn and spiteful man - one moreover too foolish to realise that such qualities were not suitable for kingship. He had used the kingdom as if it were some great toy in the hands of a boy, not a treasure in the hands of a man. Wake and d'Ayville can have had no illusions about the fate that awaited them as rebels, the sons of rebels, if they had nothing with which to bargain.

But Derby was a great magnate with contacts, wealth and power. It was he who had raised the rebellion, he who had brought men to his standard and he who had the vision of what needed to be done. With him at their sides, Wake and d'Ayville may yet have been able to succeed in their rising, but without him the rebellion was doomed. Even if the rebellion were defeated anyway, Derby could at least use his bargaining power to save their lives and perhaps a portion of their lands.

It must have seemed that everything hinged on Derby. But where was he?

After hanging around in the fields outside Chesterfield for some time, Wake and d'Ayville decided to go looking for Derby. That meant going back into Chesterfield. Having only just been driven out of the town at swordpoint this was a bold move, but one that the two commanders must have felt was worth a try.

A scene in New Beetwell Street, Chesterfield. It is unlikely that the final rebel assault got as far as this since it was on the far western end of the town in 1266. However, some fighting may have taken place here.

The attack began at midnight. So far as we can tell the gates were closed this time, so the troops scrambled up the earthworks, clambered over the wooden pallisade and then stormed into the darkened town. It seems to have been d'Ayville who led the assault, or at least it was to him that the men looked for leadership. Again the fighting was confused and brutal. The streets were now quite dark with only the faintest of light showing the attackers where to go and what to do.

In similar circumstances other medieval commanders gave their men a distinguishing mark to wear so that they could tell friend from foe. White cloth armbands would have made sense on such a dark night, but we do not know what d'Ayville used. That he had some sort of recognition signal is clear for his men were well able to recognise each other.

The attack seems to have gone in from the south or the southeast, though we cannot be certain. Henry of Almain was caught off guard, but not so completely by surprise as had been Wake and Derby. His men were pushed back through the town, but quickly rallied and began forming up within the narrow streets. The attacking rebels had got as far as the market place, but they could get no further. Either on orders of Henry or on their own initiative royal troops began setting fire to the houses of Chesterfield. The houses were of wood with thatched roofs, so once set firmly alight they burned well, and brightly. The bright flames of hundreds of tons of wood going up cast a bright light over the scene. By the light of the burning houses, the royalists began pushing the rebels back. D'Ayville did his best, but it was no use. Once the rebel soldiers realised that they were once again being pushed back they turned and fled.

Running pell mell back over the walls and down the slope, the rebels again drew breath in the fields a mile or so from the town. Nothing had been gained by attack, except more dead bodies and several houses going up in flames. Wake and d'Ayville still did not know where Derby was. They had, however, done their best. Now all that remained for them to do was to go home and await their fates.

When dawn came it revealed a dark cloud of smoke still hanging over Chesterfield as the burning houses smouldered on. To the north Wake and d'Ayville and their men were trailing off back to Lincolnshire and Yorkshire. In the town the royalist soldiers and townsfolk were putting out the fires. Although a wooden house will burn well enough when set on fire, the flames will not spread as easily to neighbouring properties as is generally assumed, especially after rain. Damp thatch does not burn so cinders falling on to roofs will not catch fire and flames will not spread through walls unless encouraged to do so by openenings. Whether it had rained recently or not we do not know, but the flames did not spread rapidly and by midmorning they were under control.

However, Henry of Almain had no more idea of where Derby was than had Wake or d'Ayville. He had learned from prisoners taken in the midnight fighting that the reason for the assault had been to rescue Derby, so he knew that Derby was not with the rebels. Henry ordered that all the dead bodies and all the wounded be brought to the market square where he could inspect them and see if Derby were amongst them. He was not.

Next Henry again summoned the city officials. This time he told them that he was looking for the Earl of Derby. Henry adopted a carrot and stick approach. He offered a large reward if Derby were to be handed over, but also promised to tear the town apart and set fire to every building if he were not. Within minutes the word of the huge reward reached the ears of the young woman who worked

A modern re-enactor dressed as a herald. The aftermath of any medieval battle was a time for the heralds. It was generally heralds who were expected to identify the dead, but they also collected stories of the actions of nobles and knights so that the tale of the battle could be turned into songs or poems, and the main details recorded by chroniclers.
With thanks to the Medieval Combat Society.

in the doctor's surgery beside the church. It was to here that Derby had come seeking relief from his gout and he had still been there when the attack by the royalists had begun. The young woman knew exactly where Derby was hiding because she had shown him the hiding place herself.

After assuring herself that she would indeed get the reward, the woman led a troop of soldiers to the church and into a group of storage sheds that then stood adjacent to the churchyard wall. In these sheds were stored several large bales of wool that had come in from farms on the Derbyshire hills ready to be sold at the great Whitsuntide Fair. Derby, she said, was hiding behind the bales in a small alcove, and so he was.

Derby was dragged in front of Henry, who treated him with every courtesy but made it very clear that he was a prisoner and would remain so. Derby was put under armed guard and sent south to Windsor Castle to await King Henry's decision. Henry of Almain, meanwhile, mustered his men and set off in pursuit of Wake and d'Ayville.

It was noon on 16 May 1266 and the Battle of Chesterfield was over.

The sequence of events outlined above is not accepted by all historians. The contemporary chronicles record a number of individual details, but do not give a consistent chronology of the battle. Some historians believe that the fight between d'Ayville's column and Henry of Almain's men in which d'Ayville was unhorsed took place after the night fighting and as d'Ayville was retreating back the way he had come. Others have located the rally of Wake and d'Ayville to the west or south of the town, or even to the north. Such confusion is not unusual for medieval battles for the chroniclers were much more interested in the causes and results of such events than their conduct.

When events of a battle are mentioned it is much more usual to find chroniclers talking about the prowess, or otherwise, of individual knights and nobles. After all, it was these knights and nobles who might want to buy a copy of the chronicle, or at least a shortened version of it that mentions them, or to become patrons of the writer.

CHAPTER 6
AFTERMATH

Robert de Ferrers, Earl of Derby, was put before a court by King Henry III at Windsor later in 1266. As everyone expected he was found guilty of high treason, sentenced to death and all his lands and estates confiscated. The lands were handed over to Edmund, second son of King Henry III who was also given the title of Earl of Derby.

However, that was not the end of things. Although the rising in Derbyshire had been put down by the Battle of Chesterfield, other rebels were still in the field. One such group was holed up in the powerful Kenilworth Castle in Warwickshire. Prince Edward marched on Kenilworth himself, but the castle proved impossible to capture by assault. Edward settled down to starve the rebel garrison into surrender before moving on to Ely and Axholme, where other rebel forces were holding out.

But in August the Church decided to take a hand. As was usual in the middle ages, it was the Church that sought to bring peace between kings and barons, which sought to ease suffering during famines or outbreaks of disease and, as at Kenilworth, to stop bloodshed by finding a mutually agreeable solution to a violent quarrel. The Pope himself had sent a legate, Cardinal Ottobuono Fieschi, to try to halt the fighting between King Henry III and Simon de Montfort. By the time the legate arrived Simon was dead, but he was able to open talks between Edward and the rebels inside Kenilworth.

Fiescki persuaded Edward and the rebels to appoint representatives to meet under his chairmanship and under the protection of the Church to try to thrash out terms. Edward said he would wait until 1 November, but if no agreement were reached by then the siege would begin again. A deal was finally struck at the very last minute, on 31 October. The agreement, soon dubbed "the Dictum of Kenilworth" proved to be the template by which peace was made by all the rebels and the king. It was subscribed to by Ferrers of Derby from his prison cell.

Under the terms of the Dictum of Kenilworth, the rebels were to be restored to

44

their titles and estates on condition that they paid a hefty fine. Those who had supported the rebellion without marching to war had to pay a fine equivalent to twice the annual income from their estates. Those who had gone to war had to pay five times their annual income, Leaders, such as Derby, had to pay seven times. The money had to be paid immediately and since no medieval nobleman had that sort of money lying about it meant that the rebels had to borrow the money to pay their fines. The loans were then paid back over coming years out of the rents and other income.

Kenilworth Castle was besieged by the royalists for months in 1266 without success. The walls of the Great Tower (on the right) are 17 feet thick and almost 100 feet high. By the standards of the 13th century this fortress was impregnable to all weapons except starvation.

It was a clever agreement on Edward's part, but only one section of the overall peace deal. Edward was wise enough to recognise his father's faults and had some sympathy with the aims of the rebels, though not with their means. He also knew that he would soon be king himself and that he would have to rule over these people. By imposing on the rebels a hefty fine he allowed them to keep their dignity, titles and estates - all the things that made life worth living for a medieval nobleman - but condemned them to years of penury. So long as the former rebels were paying over a large proportion of their income to repay the debts, they would not have enough money left to fund a rebellion.

Edward also made sure that many of the demands of the rebels were met once the fighting was over. Parliament met regularly, the king was subject to the law of the land and nobles were given a prominent role in the affairs of state. He laid the foundations that made England a united and powerful kingdom for more than a century, when another foolish king made a mess of things.

Derby agreed to the Dictum of Kenilworth, but he was not to enjoy its benefits. Prince Edmund kidnapped him and held him prisoner until he had agreed to hand over his lands. Edmund then used the estates as collatoral to raise funds to recruit an army and take it on crusade to the Holy Land. When Derby got free, Edmund had gone. Derby spent most of the rest of his life trying to get his lands back. He tried legal actions and he tried grabbing them by force, but it was not to be. In 1275 he managed to get back his mother's dowry lands on the grounds that they had been left in trust to Derby's children and so did not really belong to him and could not be confiscated. After Derby's death in 1279 his widow extracted a cash payment from Edmund in lieu of some other estates.

After Chesterfield, Wake and d'Ayville went to join the rebels holding out on the Isle of Axholme, led by Simon de Montfort's son, also Simon. The area then really was an island, surrounded by extensive marshes and swamps which have since been drained. They remained there until they agreed to the Dictum of Kenilworth and went home. Wake died in 1281, d'Ayville's date of death is unknown.

Henry of Almain joined Prince Edmund on the crusade financed by the lands stolen from Derby. But when the crusaders reached Sicily, Henry was ordered by Edward to divert to Gascony. Gascony was then owned by the English crown, but there was trouble and Edward wanted Henry to sort it out. Henry took ship to Italy, travelling overland, taking the opportunity to visit Rome on the way.

Leaving Rome, Henry moved on to Viterbo. It was now March 1271 and as the 13th was a Sunday Henry went to attend mass in the Church of San Silvestro. As he was entering the church, Henry by sheer chance bumped into Simon de Montfort the younger and his brother Guy, who were now living in exile in Italy. Simon whipped out a dagger and Henry fled. Simon caught up with him at the high altar. Henry grabbed the altar cloth and begged for mercy. "You had no mercy on my father," replied Guy whereupon Simon stabbed Henry in the chest, causing his almost immediate death. Having shed blood in a church, Simon and Guy were instantly excommunicated. Simon died later that year, but Guy enrolled as a mercenary captain with Charles of Anjou. He prospered and married a minor heiress, through whom he became Count of Nola. He died in 1288.

Ottobuono Fieschi went on to become Pope Adrian V, though he occupied the papal throne for only six weeks in 1276 before he died.

The tomb of Pope Adrian V who, as Cardinal Ottobuono Fieschi, came to England in 1266 to broker a peace deal between King Henry III and his rebellious subjects. The tomb stands in the Church of San Francesco alla Rocco in Viterbo. Ironically Adrian died and was buried in the same town where the last murderous act in the cycle of revenge played out after the Battle of Chesterfield took place in 1271.

The author (right) with a modern re-enactor dressed in the armour of a 14th century knight. With thanks to the Medieval Combat Society.

ALSO AVAILABLE IN THIS SERIES

The Battle of Wimbledon 568
The Battle of Lincoln 1141
The Battle of Chesterfield 1266
The Battle of Northampton 1460
The Battle of Losecoat Field 1470
The Sieges of Newark 1643-46
The Siege of Leicester 1645